A Boy Name Same

By LaKay

First, I would like to thank God; who has made this moment possible. I would like to thank my Dad, Willie E. Roberson, for his never-ending support. Thanks also to my loving husband, Glenn McKinney, my children, my sister Dafrie, my brother Julius, my niece DaJonitta, Dr. Karen Maness for always taking time to listen to my stories offering encouragement, and everyone else who has worked so diligently to help make my dream a reality. I dedicate this book to my deceased grandmother Elizer Roberson.

Pictures: by Thaddeus McKinney

This book was written to encourage children and young adults to have confidence in themselves and build self-esteem.

A Boy Name Same

In the city of Richwood, there lived a boy named Peter. He lived with his mother, father, and two sisters. He went to a school called Richwood Junior High. Peter was a nice child who never got into trouble. Peter's only flaw was that he sometimes did not like to take out the trash, clean his room, or cut the grass. That was not so bad, because most boys his age did not like to do that kind of work either. Most of the time he liked to sit in his room and play on the computer.

There were all kinds of activities for children to do after school, but Peter would not participate in these events. He was just too shy. He always wanted to play football, but he thought he was not good enough. He also wanted to play basketball but again he thought he was not good enough. It seemed like every time he wanted to do something, he would always get a terrible feeling. He would think that he could not do it or HE WAS NOT GOOD ENOUGH!

One day Peter found out that a group of children were starting a dance group. This made him so excited, because he loved to dance. This group would be known as the Step Team. Since Peter loved dancing so much, he decided to go watch the team practice. As he watched them, he paid close attention to every step. He went home and practiced every day, until he became really good. Now, anytime Peter was not on the computer, he was dancing through the house.

Peter soon realized that it was only two weeks until the tryouts for the Step Team. Peter started spending more time in his room with the door closed, so no one could watch him practice. On the evening before his tryout fear began to creep in, and Peter began having second thoughts about trying out. Peter felt all alone. He was really hurting this time, because he loved dancing so much. Peter decided that he was not going to try out, even though making the team would be like a dream come true.

Peter's mother, father, nor sisters knew what Peter was going through. He was so sad. Later that night, Peter sat in his bedroom and cried for what seemed to be hours. Suddenly, a boy appeared in his room and said, "Hello Peter."

Peter looked up and asked, "Who are you and how did you get in my room? Did my mom let you in?" The boy answered, "No." "What is your name?" Peter asked. The boy replied, "My name is Same, and I came to talk to you. Why are you crying?" The boy asked.

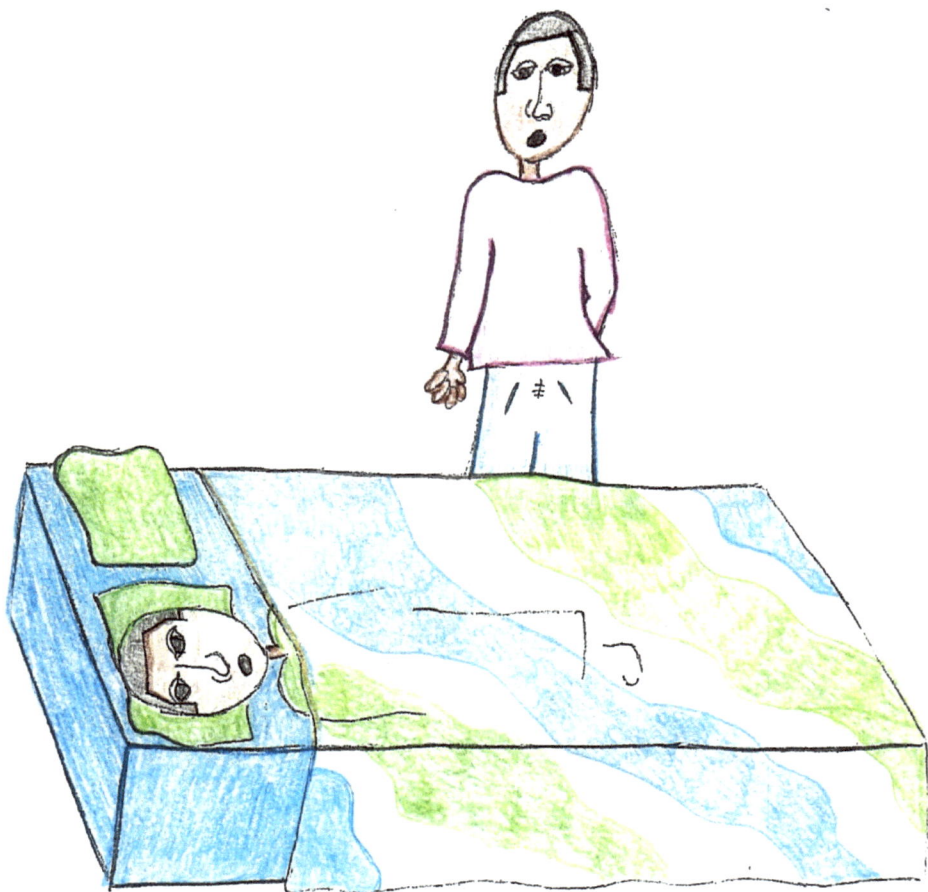

Peter said he did not feel like talking about it. Same said, "Why not?" Peter answered by saying, "I never tell anyone what is going on with me. I always keep it to myself. I feel like no one understands me, but me." Same asked, "Do you feel like you are alone sometimes?" Peter looked at Same with those sad eyes and said "Yes, sometimes I do. I wonder why I have to feel this way." Peter asked. Then Same said, "You are not alone. There are a lot of girls and boys that feel the same way you do. This happens all the time."

Peter said, "I see lots of guys playing football and basketball and it looks like they don't have any problems. I get very nervous when I have to stand in front of the class to talk about things, because I am too shy. I always want to talk about fun things with other kids, like some of the other guys do. I just always feel like it will not come out the right way, so I just don't say anything."

Same told Peter, "Those same guys that you see playing basketball and football feel the same way you do at times." "You are right! It does seem like they don't have any problems. That is the way it is supposed to look, but everyone goes through something inside. Some people can just get over their fears sooner than others." "Most people are harder on themselves than anyone else is. Would you believe that moms and dads feel the same way you do at one time or another?" Moms and dads? Peter responded.

"Yes, even TV stars." Same replied.

"Peter, you are never alone. That is why you should talk to your mom and dad. You might realize that they really do understand you. You should never cry in your room alone! If you are feeling sad, tell your parents. They were once your age too. They would not want you to worry about something and not tell them about it. They love you! They know that you are not perfect, and they are not either. They would never want you to give up on something that you really want to do." After the boy had been sitting and talking to Peter for a while, Peter began to feel very comfortable with him. Same began to talk about things no one else knew. Same also told Peter, that they both shared the same thoughts. Within those few hours of talking, the two became the best of friends. Then, Same told Peter, "You should try out for the Step Team."

Peter said, "The dancers are really good; I probably will not be chosen."

Then Same said, "You are just as good as the rest of them. Those guys have to learn the routine also.

They are no different than you." So, are you going to try out?" Same asked. Peters said, "I feel so comfortable with you. I want you to be there with me." Then Same said, "You can do it! You have the power within you that you need! You already have it! Do not let your fears stop you. So what if you feel pressure! Everyone does when they get excited."

"So, are you going to try out?" Same asked again. "What if I don't make it?" Peter asked. "At least you can try out. If you don't make it, you can try again later." Same replied.

Peter asked Same to promise him that he would be there. So Same promised. Now, Peter felt that he had the courage to try out.

Peter was a still a little bit nervous the following day, but he kept telling himself that he could do it. He became more and more nervous as he watched the tryouts and saw how good the people performing were. Immediately, he began to look for the boy, but did not see him.

When the person just before Peter began performing, he thought to himself, "He is a great dancer." He looked for the boy again but did not see him. Then the announcer called Peter's name. Peter was very scared but then remembered what the boy had told him. He tried his very best. When the tryouts were over Peter's name was announced for making the team. Peter was so happy! He looked for Same again, but he did not see him. He wanted him to be there, but Same was nowhere to be found. Peter did not know why Same did not show up, but he was still happy!

When Peter made it home and told his parents about the contest, they were very happy for him. While they ate supper at the dinner table, his mother wondered why Peter did not tell them about the tryouts.

"Why didn't you let us know that you were going to try out?" His dad asked. "Yeah, we enjoy watching you dance." His mother said. Peter told them that he didn't know how to express his feelings, because he felt like no one would understand him. Peter began to explain. "A boy came in my room and began to talk to me."

"What? A boy came into your room."
His mother asked.

Peter said "Yes, and I did not even know him."

"What was his name Peter?" His mother asked.

"Same."

"Same?" She said.

"Yes, that's what he told me," Peter said. "Were you dreaming?" She asked. "No, Mom, I was in my room crying. He came in and we started talking." Then she told Peter, "You should have talked to us. Never go through anything alone!" "Yes Ma'am," said Peter. Peter told his parents good night and went to his room for bed. After he lay in bed for a while the boy appeared again.

"Hello Peter." Same said.

"Hi!," Peter said excitedly.

"I made it! I made it! I am so happy.

I made it. Can you believe it?"

"I can believe it." Same said. "I knew you could do it!"

Peter said, "I wanted you there and I was really disappointed when I didn't see you."

Then Same turned to Peter and said, "I was there when you were looking around for me."

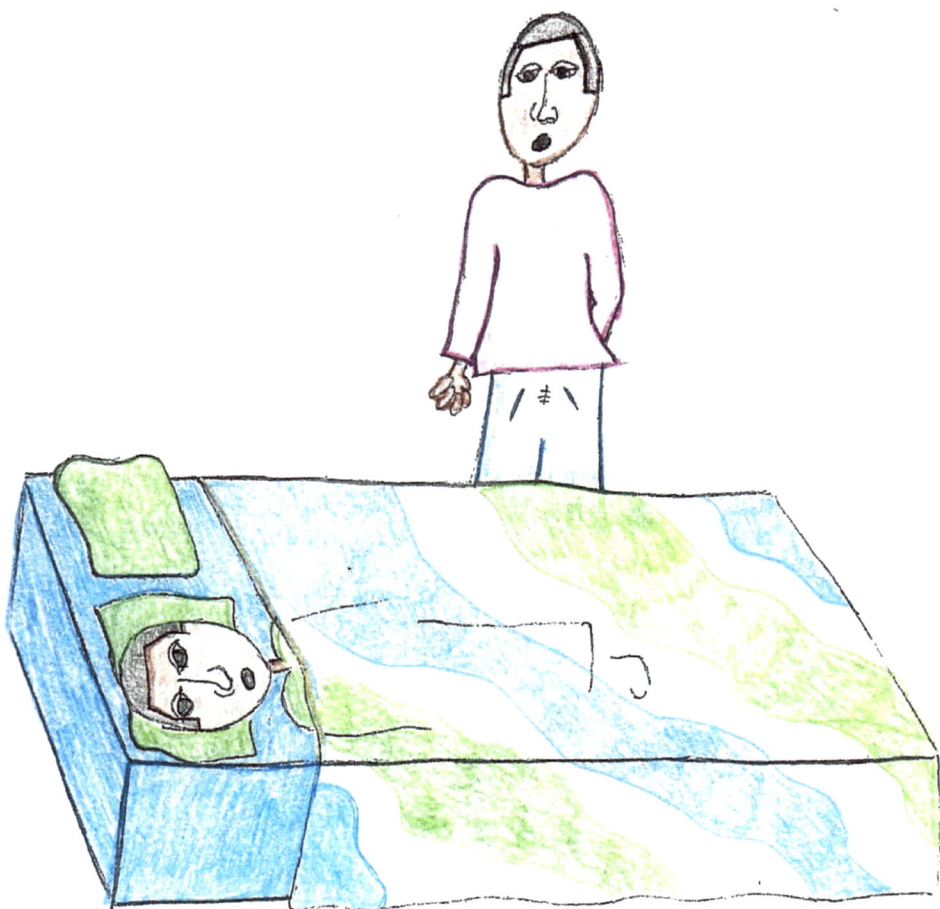

"I was there when the person dancing just before you was called to come onto the stage, and you thinking how good he was. I was also there when you were really nervous. I was there the whole time. Everything you went through, I went through it with you."

"I didn't see you," Peter said.

"I know," said Same, "but I was there."

Peter asked, "Why are you trying to make me think that you were there, and I know that I didn't see you there?"

"Well," said Same, "Take a good look at me and listen. My hair is the same as yours. Our eyes are also the same. Whenever you say, I do not think I can. I say, "I know you can. I am the part of you that is positive, and I see all of the good things in you. Whenever you doubt that you can do something; I am, telling you that you can do it. I am the voice that everyone has inside of them. You just have to release your fears and believe that whatever someone else can do, you can do also. You should try until you reach your goals, and always remember I will be right there. I will never leave you."

After really listening to Same that night, I began to have more confidence and I was happier with myself. I wasn't as shy anymore, nor did I get as nervous when competing against others. Whenever I had a problem, I didn't hesitate to go to my parents or pull out the power within from Same. I now realize I am Same. His name is the same as mine!

From time to time, everyone needs help in one way or another.

Sometimes, we don't always seek the right people to get advice from. I hope after reading this book, the reader will be able to get in touch with their true, inner self, and learn the importance of communicating with their parents.

www.ingramcontent.com/pod-product-compliance
Lightning Source LLC
Chambersburg PA
CBHW041817040426
42452CB00001B/7